Editor
Gisela Lee, M.A.

Managing Editor
Karen Goldfluss, M.S. Ed.

Editor-in-Chief
Sharon Coan, M.S. Ed.

Illustrator
Sue Fullam

Cover Artist
Barb Lorseyedi

Art Coordinator
Kevin Barnes

Art Director
CJae Froshay

Imaging
Temo Parra

Product Manager
Phil Garcia

Publisher
Mary D. Smith, M.S. Ed.

Math Games

GRADE 4

Practice Makes Perfect

Author

Mary Rosenberg

Teacher Created Resources, Inc.
6421 Industry Way
Westminster, CA 92683
www.teachercreated.com
ISBN: 978-0-7439-3721-4
©2003 Teacher Created Resources, Inc.
Reprinted, 2008
Made in U.S.A.

Table of Contents

Introduction and Materials List 3

Playing Board (reproducible template). 4

Game 1: Number Match 5

Game 2: Neighbors 6

Game 3: Five-in-a-Row 7

Game 4: Four-in-a-Row. 8

Game 5: Build a Number Line 9

Game 6: "Egg"-xactly Right. 10

Game 7: Making Numbers 11

Game 8: Give Me Twenty! 12

Game 9: Coins-in-a-Row. 13

Game 10: Take the Money. 14

Game 11: Put It in the Bank 15

Game 12: Who Did It? 16

Game 13: Addition Bingo 18

Game 14: Subtraction Bingo 19

Game 15: Hang Ten. 20

Game 16: Draw a Cat 21

Game 17: Ten Squares. 22

Game 18: Cat and Mouse 23

Game 19: The Banker 24

Game 20: Number Flip 25

Game 21: Shapes Rule! 26

Game 22: Don't Be Late! 26

Game 23: Penny Toss 29

Game 24: Rolling Numbers. 30

Game 25: Hundreds of Riddles 31

Game 26: Graph Art 31

Game 27: Math Art 36

Game 28: Logic Problems 38

Game 29: Patterns 41

Game 30: Can You Find the Mistake?. 41

Game 31: Shhh! Say It in Code #1 45

Game 32: Build a House 47

Answer Key 48

❧ Introduction and Materials List ❧

Introduction

The games and activities in *Practice Makes Perfect: Math Games (Grade 1)* focus on important math skills that every first grader needs to learn. Many of the games can be played with only one player or with a partner and use many items commonly found in the home. The games provide review and practice in the following areas of math:

- adding
- subtracting
- counting
- telling time
- counting money
- shapes
- coordinate points
- place value
- patterns
- logical thinking
- number words

Many of the games do not have just one right answer. This allows children of all different abilities and ages to play the games together (and with adults) for hours of enjoyment and success.

Most of the games can be played in multiple ways and can be "custom tailored" to meet the child's needs just by changing the numbers being added or subtracted, by changing a manipulative part (spinner, dice, number cards), or by using different numbers on the playing board.

Materials List

The games in this book can be played using items commonly found in the home. The items include:

- playing cards
- counters—beans, pennies, nickels, dimes, paper clips
- 3" x 5" blank index cards or small squares of scratch paper
- 1" graph paper
- stamp pad
- stamps
- magazines
- dice
- scissors
- small stickers
- double-six dominoes
- pencils
- crayons
- glue sticks
- checkers
- small sticky notes
- egg cartons

Have the children become active participants in the learning process. If game cards need to be made, have the child make the cards using crayons, markers, stickers, stamps, or pictures cut from magazines. Store each set of cards in a plastic sandwich bag. Use a label to note the items stored inside each plastic sandwich bag.

Many of these game pieces can be used to play a variety of games. Once the game pieces are made, store each set of cards in a small plastic sandwich bag and keep the game pieces in a shoebox. This will also make the games "portable"—they can be played just about anywhere there is a flat surface.

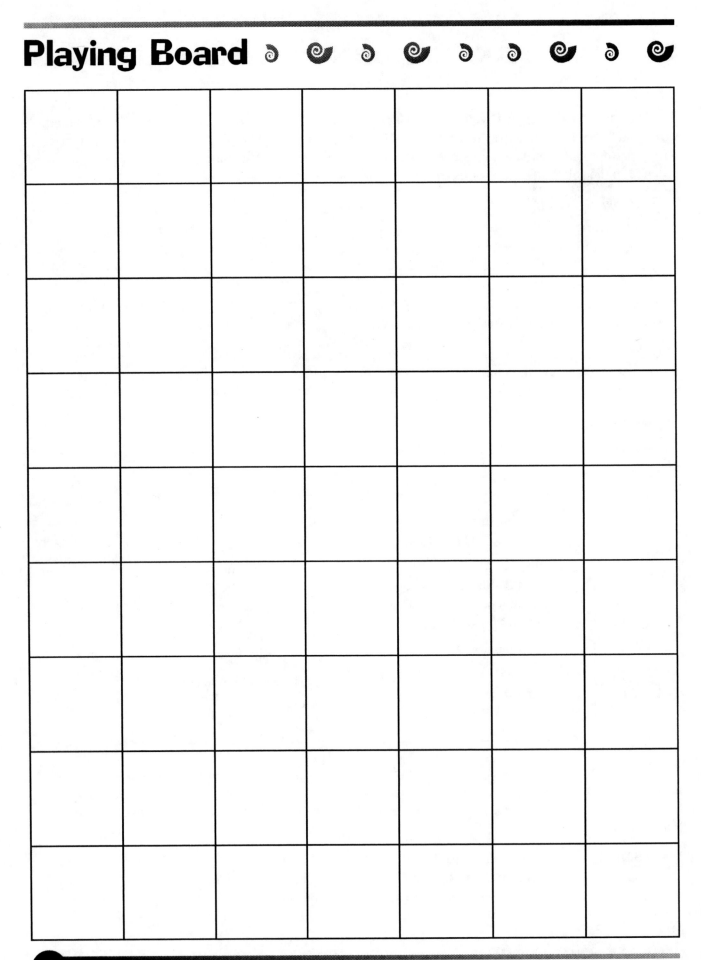

Game 1

Number Match

Number of Players: 1 or more

Skills

- reading numbers to ten

- reading number words to ten

- counting to ten

Materials

- 33 blank 3" x 5" index cards (Write the numerals 0–10, write the number words zero to ten and draw pictures or stamp pictures to show 0–10 items on each individual card.)

Object of the Game

- to match pictures, numbers, and number words

Directions

- Lay the cards face up on a table in a 3 x 3 arrangement.

- Taking turns, the first player looks for two cards that match—example, the word "three" and the numeral "3." After the player has picked up all of the cards that match, fill in the empty spaces in the 3 x 3 arrangement with the remaining cards. (Note: If there are no matching cards in the first 3 x 3 arrangement, reshuffle the cards in with the remaining cards in the deck and arrange another set.)

- The second player may have his or her turn to find all the matches.

- Continue in this manner until there are no cards left. Then, have the players place the 11 card sets in order from 0 to 10. (The sequence will have a mix of pictures, number words, and numerals.)

Game 2 ꙮ ꙮ ꙮ ꙮ ꙮ ꙮ ꙮ ꙮ ꙮ ꙮ ꙮ

Neighbors

Number of Players: 2

Skill: identifying the number that comes before or after a given number

Materials

- one (or more) set of playing cards with the face cards removed or use 40 blank 3" x 5" index cards and write four sets of numbers 1–10

Object of the Game

- to make as many "neighbors" as possible

Directions

- Shuffle the cards and deal five cards to each player. Place the remaining cards in a stack face down on the table.

- Each player looks through his or her cards and removes any neighbors (successive numbers). The player then picks up cards from the stack until he or she is holding five cards again. Each player repeats this step until he or she is holding cards that do not have any "neighbors."

- Each player should always have five cards in his or her hand.

- Taking turns, one player asks, "Do you have any neighbors for 9?" If the other player has, he or she either says, "Yes, I have an 8 (or a 10)" and hands the card to the player. The player removes the 9 from his or her hand and picks replacement cards from the stack, or if the other player does not have a neighbor, he or she says, "Sorry, go on a number hunt." (The player takes the top card from the stack.)

- Play continues in this manner until all of the cards have been used or there aren't any more neighbors. The winner has the most neighbor cards.

Player One

Neighbors are 7 and 8.

Player Two

Neighbors are 1 and 2 and 4 and 5.

(Players actually hold their cards so that only they can see the numbers.)

Game 3 ᔆ ❧ ᔆ ❧ ᔆ ❧ ᔆ ᔆ ❧ ᔆ ❧

Five-in-a-row

Number of Players: 2–4

Skills

- counting from 0–5
- reading the number words zero to five

Materials

- playing board (page 4) or 1" graph paper with the numbers 0–5 placed randomly on the playing board
- 20 blank 3" x 5" index cards labeled with the number words zero to five or stamped showing 0–5 items on each card. (Stickers can also be used on the cards.)
- different set of counters for each player

Object of the Game

- to be the first player to have five counters in a row

Directions

- Taking turns, each player turns over the top card. The player counts the number of items stamped on the cards or reads the number word. The player places a counter on the corresponding number on the playing board.
- Play continues in this manner until somebody has five counters in a row. (**Note:** If no one has won after the card stack is depleted, shuffle the cards and reuse the stack until a winner is selected.)

Variations

- On 21 blank 3" x 5" index cards write the following addition problems. (Stamps can also be used in place of the numerals.)

0 + 0	0 + 1	0 + 2	0 + 3	0 + 4	0 + 5	1 + 0	1 + 1	1 + 2	1 + 3	1 + 4
2 + 0	2 + 1	2 + 2	2 + 3	3 + 0	3 + 1	3 + 2	4 + 0	4 + 1	5 + 0	

Taking turns, each player turns over the top card, reads the math problem, and places a counter on the answer found on the playing board.

- On 21 blank 3" x 5" index cards, write the following subtraction problems. (Stamps with items crossed out can also be used in place of the numerals.)

5 – 0	5 – 1	5 – 2	5 – 3	5 – 4	5 – 5	4 – 0	4 – 1	4 – 2	4 – 3	4 – 4
3 – 0	3 – 1	3 – 2	3 – 3	2 – 0	2 – 1	2 – 2	1 – 0	1 – 1	0 – 0	

Taking turns, each player turns over the top card, reads the math problem, and places a counter on the answer found on the playing board.

- For a more challenging game, play the game using both sets of addition and subtraction math problems. Play the game following the same directions outlined above.

Game 4 🐚 🐚 🐚 🐚 🐚 🐚 🐚 🐚 🐚 🐚 🐚

Four-in-a-Row

Number of Players: 1–2

Skills

- counting to 12
- adding to 12
- subtracting to 12

Materials

- playing board (page 4) with the numbers 0–12 placed randomly on the board or 1" graph paper
- different set of counters for each player
- one set of double-six dominoes

Object of the Game

- to be the first player to have four counters in a row

Directions

- Taking turns, each player turns over a domino, counts the total number of pips (dots), and places a counter on the corresponding number. The first player to have four counters in a row wins the game.

Variations

- On 20 blank 3" x 5" index cards, write four sets of the number words *six, seven, eight, nine,* and *ten.* Write the numbers 6–12 randomly on the playing board. Shuffle the cards and place in a stack facedown on the table. Taking turns, each player turns over the top number card, reads the number word, and places a counter on the corresponding number. The first player to have four counters in a row wins the game.

- On 56 blank 3" x 5" index cards, write two sets of the following addition problems:

6 + 0	6 + 1	6 + 2	6 + 3	6 + 4	6 + 5	6 + 6	7 + 0	7 + 1	7 + 2
7 + 3	7 + 4	7 + 5	8 + 0	8 + 1	8 + 2	8 + 3	8 + 4	9 + 0	9 + 1
9 + 2	9 + 3	10 + 0	10 + 1	10 + 2	11 + 0	11 + 1	12 + 0		

Label the playing board using the numbers 6–12. Play the game as outlined above.

- On 56 blank 3" x 5" index cards, write two sets of the following subtraction problems:

12 − 0	12 − 1	12 − 2	12 − 3	12 − 4	12 − 5	12 − 6	11 − 0	11 − 1	11 − 2
11 − 3	11 − 4	11 − 5	10 − 0	10 − 1	10 − 2	10 − 3	10 − 4	9 − 0	9 − 1
9 − 2	9 − 3	8 − 0	8 − 1	8 − 2	7 − 0	7 − 1	6 − 0		

Label the playing board using the numbers 6–12. Play the game as outlined above.

- For a more challenging game, play the game using both sets of addition and subtraction math problems. Play the game following the same directions outlined above.

Game 5

Build a Number Line

Number of Players: 2

Skill: identifying the number that comes before or after a specific number

Materials

* one set of playing cards with the face cards removed or use 3"x 5" index cards and write the numbers 1–10

Object of the Game

* to be the first player to use all of the cards

Directions

* Mix the cards on the tabletop. Each player selects five cards. Turning the cards faceup, the player with the 5 card goes first, placing the card in the middle of the table. The next player must play either the card that comes before (4) or after (6). If this player does not have the card that comes before or after, the other player plays one of the appropriate cards (either the 4 or 6 card) Game continues in this manner until one player has used all of his or her cards.

Variations

* A different range of numbers can be used—for example the numbers 0–15. Before playing the game, decide which card needs to be in the middle (in this case either card 7 or 8 before playing the game.

* Dominoes can be used to play this game. Just pull out the dominoes with the pips for 0–12. The player with the 6 or 7 goes first.

(Cards are actually held so that each player can see only his or her cards.)

Game 6 ᵔ ᵕ ᵔ ᵕ ᵔ ᵕ ᵔ ᵔ ᵕ ᵔ ᵕ

"Egg"-xactly Right

Number of Players: 1 or more

Skill: counting to 12

Materials

- one egg carton for each player (Use the numbers 1–12 to number each space of the carton. If using a die, have the players place a counter in the 1 space.)
- one set of double-six dominoes or two six-sided dice

Object of the Game

- to be the first player to fill all of the egg spaces with a counter in each

Directions

- Taking turns, each player picks a domino (or rolls both dice), counts the pips, and places a counter in the matching space in the egg carton. Once a space has been used, it cannot be used again.
- The first player to fill all of the egg spaces wins the game.

Variations

- Using 3" x 5" index cards, write addition and/or subtraction problems for which the sum or difference is between 0 and 13.. Use sticky notes to relabel each egg space. Taking turns, have each player turn over a card, solve the problem, and place a counter in the corresponding egg space.
- Have the players relabel their egg cartons using their favorite numbers. (If a child chooses, he or she may use the same number several times. For example: 3, 7, 6, 9, 6, 5, 8, 10, 3, 3, 8, 5.) Have the players play the game as outlined above.

Game 7

Making Numbers

Number of Players: 1 or more

Skills

- place value (tens and ones)
- identifying odd and even numbers

Materials

- one set of playing cards with the face cards and the 10's removed
- spinner
- paper clip
- pencil
- paper (optional)

Object of the Game

- to have a number fit a specific criteria

Directions

- Evenly divide the cards among all players. At the same time, all players turn over the top two cards and say what number they make when placed side by side.
- Taking turns, one player spins the spinner using a paper clip as the "arrow" and a pencil to hold the paperclip in the middle of the circle. The student with the number that fits the criteria wins and takes the two cards. (If desired, the player can record the number he or she made on a piece of paper. A number that has been circled designates that he or she won that particular round.) If both players make numbers that fit the criteria, the player with the higher number wins the round.
- Play continues in this manner, with all children taking turns spinning the spinner.
- The player who ends up with all of the cards (or the most cards within a given time frame) wins the game.

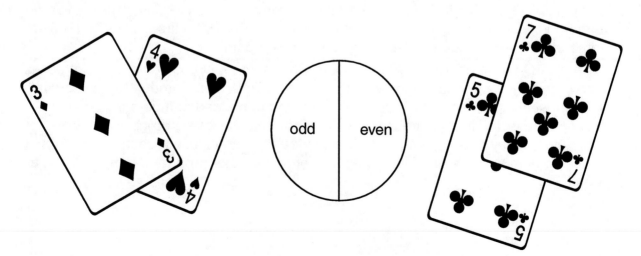

Game 8 ✺ ✺ ✺ ✺ ✺ ✺ ✺ ✺ ✺ ✺ ✺

Give Me Twenty!

Number of Players: 2–4

Skill: counting to 20

Materials

- playing board (page 4) or a piece of 1" graph paper
- 20 counters for each player
- one six-sided die or a set of playing cards removing the numbers 7–10 and the face cards

Object of the Game

- to be the first player to get rid of all of his or her counters

Directions

- Give each player 20 counters. (For this game the counters can all be the same.)
- Taking turns, each player rolls the die (or picks a card). Starting in any available space, the player places the matching number of counters on the playing board.

Examples of Playing Situations

- If a player rolls a "6" and there are only three spaces left on the playing board, the player must remove 6 counters and add them to his or her pile of counters. (In other words if a player rolls a "6," he or she must place 1 counter in 6 continuous squares.)
- If a player rolls a "6" but only has two counters, the player must remove 6 counters from the board.

Variations

For these variations, each player will need to have his or her own specific set of counters.

- The spaces on the playing board can be sequentially (or randomly) numbered 1–20. On 3" x 5" blank index cards, have the players write the numbers 1–20. Shuffle the cards and place in a stack face down on the table. Taking turns, each player turns over the top card and places a counter on the corresponding number. The first player to get 3 (or some other prearranged number) in a row wins the game.
- On a clean playing board, have the players write number words in the different boxes. (For example, the players might write the number words zero through four in several different spaces on the playing board.) Remove the needed numbers from a deck of playing cards, shuffle the cards, and place them in a stack face down on the table. Taking turns, have each player turn over the top card and place a counter on the matching number. The first player to get 3 (or some other prearranged number) in a row wins the game.

Game 9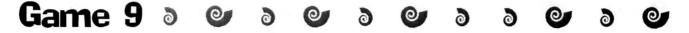

Coins-in-a-Row

Number of Players: 2–3

Skills

- logical thinking
- counting to a specific number

Materials

- playing board (page 4) or 1" graph paper (with a specific number of squares sectioned off 5 x 5, 6 x 6, 8 x 8, etc.)
- pennies, nickels, and dimes for each player (different set of coins for each player)

Object of the Game

- to be the first player to have three (or some other specified number) of coins in a row (horizontally, vertically, or diagonally)

Directions

- Taking turns, each player places one of his or her coins on the playing board. Each player wants to end up with three of his or her coins in a row and at the same time "block" the other player(s) from getting three coins in a row. The first player to get the specified number of coins in a row wins the game.
- Have the players use tally marks to keep track of the number of games each player wins.

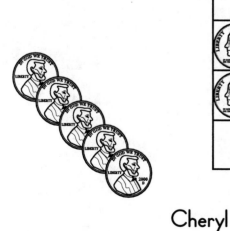
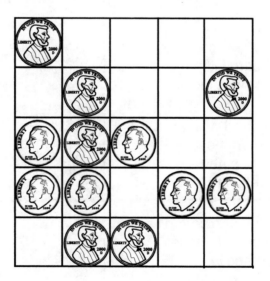

Cheryl

||||

D.J.

||

Game 10 ﾟ ♋ ﾟ ♋ ﾟ ♋ ﾟ ﾟ ♋ ﾟ ♋

Take the Money

Number of Players: 2–4

Skill: counting coins to make a specific value

Materials
- playing board (page 4) or 1" graph paper (with a specific number of squares sectioned off—5 x 5, 6 x 6, 8 x 8, etc.)
- pennies and nickels

Object of the Game
- to take the most money off of the playing board

Directions
- Before playing the game, decide what the value for that round will be, for example, 3¢, 5¢, 6¢, etc.
- Within a sectioned-off area of the playing board (or on the graph paper), lay out coins in random order, one in each space.
- Taking turns, each player removes the needed coins to make the value. The coins that are removed have to be touching on at least one side.
- When all of the coins have been removed or there are not enough coins touching on at least one side to make the specific value, the game is over. Each player counts the amount of money he or she collected. The player with the most money wins the game.

Variations
- Have the children practice skip counting by covering the playing board with nickels (counting by 5's) or with dimes (counting by 10's).
- To make the game more challenging, other coins can be placed on the playing board, such as dimes and quarters. Have the children play to a larger value, such as 39¢, 50¢, 72¢.
- Have the children roll a die (or dice) and remove the matching amount of money from the board. As noted above, all coins removed must touch on at least one side.

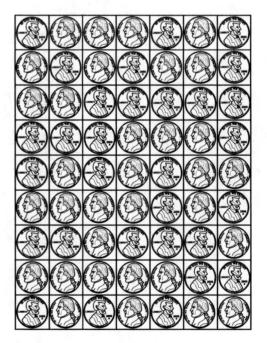

Game 11

Put It in the Bank

Number of Players: 2–3

Skills

- counting coins
- number recognition

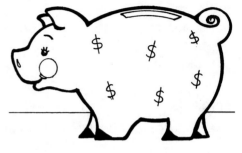

Materials

- playing board (page 4) or 1" graph paper
- 20 pennies for each player
- a six-sided die or a deck of playing cards, remove both the face cards and cards numbered 6–10

Object of the Game

- to be the first player to use all of his or her pennies

Directions

- Taking turns, each player rolls the die (or picks the playing card on the top of the deck) and places the matching number of pennies anywhere on the board.
- If a player rolls a number and there are not enough empty spaces on the board, the player does not put any coins on the board and play continues with the next player.
- If a player rolls a number and does not have enough coins, the player does not put any coins on the board and play continues with the next player.
- The player to use all of his or her coins first wins the game.

Variations

- To make the game more challenging, have the player place the coins on the playing board so that one side is touching one of the other coins he or she is using.
- The game can be made more challenging by having each player use a variety of coins (pennies, nickels, dimes, quarters) and by rolling two dice and adding the two numbers together or by picking two playing cards and adding the two numbers together.

 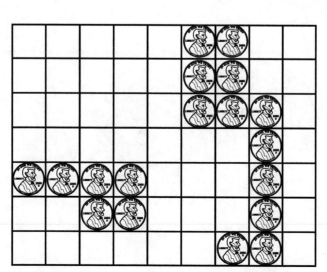

Game 12 🌀 🌀 🌀 🌀 🌀 🌀 🌀 🌀 🌀 🌀 🌀

Who Did It?

Number of Players: 2–4

Skills

- asking questions based on certain criteria

- logical thinking

Materials

- pictures of possible "suspects" from the Who Did It? activity page

- counters or sticky notes

Directions

- On a small piece of paper, the "police officer" writes the number of the culprit.

- The detective(s) or other player(s) ask the police officer questions that can be answered with "yes" or "no."

- Each detective places a counter on the person or people who fit (or do not fit) the answer.

Variations

- To make the game easier, cover one or two rows with a piece of paper so that there are fewer people for the detective to ask questions about.

- To make the game more challenging, allow the detective to ask only ten questions.

- Have the players create their own suspect boards by cutting pictures out of magazines, using stamps, or using stickers.

Game 12 *(cont.)*

Who Did It? (Pictures)

On a small piece of paper, the "police officer" writes the number of the culprit. The detective(s)—other player(s)—ask the police officer questions that can be answered with "yes" or "no." The detective places a counter on the person or people who could fit (or do not fit) the answer. To make the game easier, cover one or two rows with a piece of paper so that there are fewer people for the witness to ask questions about. To make the game more challenging, allow the witness to ask only ten questions.

1. Giggles	2. Buggy	3. Grandpa	4. Jenny	5. Bozo
6. Leo	7. Teddy	8. Tug	9. Trigger	10. Fishy
11. Kitty	12. Fishin' Bob	13. Frosty	14. Sis and Bud	15. Dudley
16. Grandma	17. Spider	18. Ben	19. Cookie	20. Dude

Game 13

Addition Bingo

Number of Players: 1–4

Skill: adding two numbers by counting

Materials

- clean sheet of paper for each player
- pencils
- number line (optional)
- one six-sided die

Object of the Game

- to be the first player to get four math problems in a row—vertically, horizontally, or diagonally

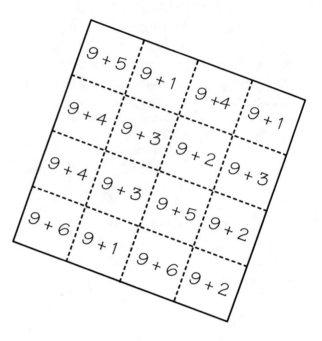

Directions

- Have each player fold a clean sheet of paper to make 16 squares. Designate a practice number (in this example, "9" is going to be used) and randomly fill each square with "9 + " and number from 0–6. Be sure to use every number from 0–6 before you repeat a number a second time.
- Taking turns, each players rolls the die. If the die lands on a "3," the player will find the math problem in which "3" was added to "9," write the sum in the box and then cover that box with a counter.
- The first player to get four math problems in a row is the winner.

Variations

- To make the game easier, have each player start each math problem with "1 + __" or "2 + __."
- Have each player write a math problem beginning with "10 + __."
- To make the game more challenging, have each player write the number sentence 12 + __ = 15 (or any other agreed upon number) using the numbers from a deck of playing cards with the face cards removed. For the missing addend, each player writes the numbers 1–10 in each square of the playing board.

Game 14

Subtraction Bingo

Number of Players: 1–4

Skill: subtracting from a given number

Materials

- clean sheet of paper for each player

- pencils

- one six-sided die

- number line (optional)

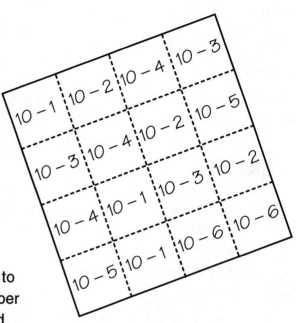

Directions

- Have each player fold a clean sheet of paper to make 16 squares. Designate a practice number (in this example, "10" is going to be used) and randomly fill each square with "10 – " and number from 0–6. Be sure to use every number from 0–6 before you repeat a number a second time.

- Taking turns, each players rolls the die. If the die lands on a "3," the player will find the math problem in which "3" was subtracted from "9," write the sum in the box and then cover that box with a counter.

- The first player to get four math problems in a row is the winner.

Variations

- Have each player write a math problem beginning with "9 – __."

- To make the game more challenging, use a deck of playing cards with the face cards removed.

- Each player writes "12 – __" (or any other agreed upon number) and completes each problem using a number from 1 to 10 in each square of the playing board.

- To make the game easier, have each player start each math problem with "6 – __" or "8 – __."

Game 15 ⟿ ❧ ⟿ ❧ ⟿ ⟿ ❧ ⟿ ⟿ ❧ ⟿ ❧

Hang Ten

Number of Players: 1–4

Skills: counting and adding to 10

Materials
- a deck of playing cards, using four sets of card numbers (1, 2, 3, and 4) and joker cards

Object of the Game
- to make a greater number than the other player(s) without going over 10

Directions
- The "dealer" gives each player one card. Starting with the player on the left, each player decides if he or she wants another card. If the player selects another card, he or she adds the two cards together. The player may choose to select another card or to "Hang Ten" or hold.
- The player who comes the closest to 10 without going over wins the round.

Variations
- Have the players keep score by using tally marks.
- Have each player keep track of the total number of points he or she earns in each round without going over ten. The first player to reach 100 wins the match.
- Players can decide to add more cards to the game and play to a larger number, such as 15 or 20.

Game 16

Draw a Cat

Number of Players: 1–4

Skill: sequential order

Materials

- scratch paper
- die or playing cards numbered 1–6

Object of the Game

- to be the first player to draw a complete cat

Directions

- Taking turns, each player rolls the die or selects a card. If the player rolls or selects a one, he or she may draw the circle (head of the cat). If the player does not roll a one, play continues with the next player. (The numbers must be rolled sequentially before the next part of the cat can be made.)

Variations

- Play using two dice and odd numbers (1, 3, 5, 7, 9, 11), even numbers (0, 2, 4, 6, 8), larger numbers (6, 7, 8, 9, 10, 11, 12), counting by 5's (5, 10, 15, 20, 25, 30), counting by 10's (10, 20, 30, 40, 50, 60), etc.
- Play the game using 3 dice and the numbers used when counting by 3's—3, 6, 9, 12, 15, 18.
- Other animals can be drawn by the players, such as a dog, elephant, mouse, hippo, bird, etc. Just make a list of the part that can be drawn for each specific number rolled.

1. Draw a circle.
2. Draw two ears.
3. Draw two eyes.
4. Add a nose.
5. Add whiskers.
6. Add the mouth.

Game 17

Ten Squares

Number of Players: 1–2

Skill: adding to 10

Materials

- 1" graph paper
- crayons—one color for each player

Object of the Game

- to color the most squares

Directions

- Taking turns, each player writes a number (0–5) on a side of a square. Each number can only be used one time within the same square. The numbers for each square needs to add up to exactly 10. The player who writes the fourth number for any given square, gets to color that square. Rotate taking turns until the board is filled. The person with the greater number of colored squares is the winner.

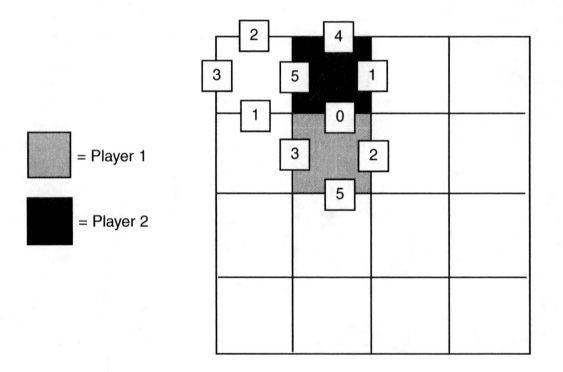

= Player 1

= Player 2

Game 18 ᨔ ᨔ ᨔ ᨔ ᨔ ᨔ ᨔ ᨔ ᨔ ᨔ ᨔ

Cat and Mouse

Number of Players: 2

Skill: introduction to coordinate points and map skills

Materials

- playing board (page 4) (Label the squares as shown below. The area can be made larger or smaller depending on how many letters and numbers are used.)
- pencils
- manila folder or some other object that can be used as a partition
- 10 small items such as pennies, beans, jelly beans, red cinnamon candies, etc., that can be used for the mice
- *optional:* graph paper labeled the same as the playing mat for the "cat" to keep track of the "houses" he has called

Object of the Game

- to catch all of the "mice"

Directions

- One person plays the "mice." The player uses a folder as a partition so the other player cannot see where the mice are being hidden. Using 10 small objects, the player hides the mice on the playing board—one mouse per square.
- The other player asks, "Is there a mouse in the house at A1?" If there is a mouse in the house at A1, the reply is "You trapped the mouse" and the mouse is handed to the cat. If there is not a mouse in the house at A1, the "mouse" replies with, "Sorry, guess again," and the cat takes another guess.
- Once all of the mice have been played, the "Cat" and the "Mouse" count how many mice each one has. The one with the most mice wins the game.

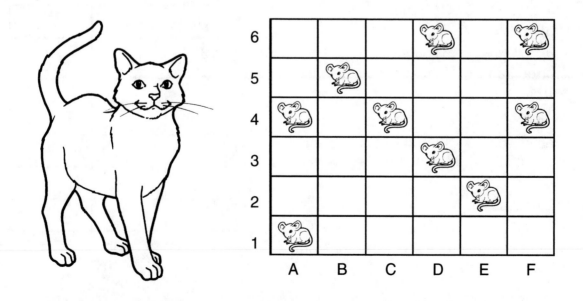

Game 19

The Banker

Number of Players: 2 or more

Skill: logical thinking

Materials
- scratch paper divided into three sections (See the example at the bottom of the page.)
- pencils

Object of the Game
- to identify the mystery number before all chances are used

Directions
- The "banker" thinks of a mystery number and writes it on a piece of paper.
- The customer(s) guess a number. The banker writes the number down on the paper and lets the customer know how many of the numbers are correct (0, 1, or 2) and how many of the numbers are in the correct place (0, 1, or 2).
- The customers take turns guessing a number, while the banker records their responses.

Sample Game

Banker writes the mystery number on a piece of paper (31).

Customer #1 guesses 25.

Banker records the guess (25) and writes 0 (numbers are correct) and 0 (numbers are in the correct place). **Note:** When 0 numbers are correct that means that those numbers are not used in the mystery number.

Customer #2 guesses 84.

Banker records the guess (84) and 0 in both columns.

Customer #3 guesses 71.

Banker records the guess (71), writes 1 (of the numbers is correct) and 1 (of the numbers is in the correct place).

Customer #4 guesses 13.

Banker records the guess (13) and writes 2 (of the numbers are correct) and 0 (of the numbers is in the correct place.)

Customer #5 guesses 31.

Banker records the guess (31) and writes 2 (of the numbers are correct and 2 (of them are in the correct place). The mystery number was 31.

0 1 ~~2~~ 3 ~~4~~ 5 ~~6~~ 7 8 9

Guess	Numbers Correct	Numbers in the Correct Place
25	0	0
84	0	0
71	1	1
13	2	0
31	2	2

Game 20

Number Flip

Number of Players: 2 or more

Skill: comparing numbers

Materials

- playing cards with the face cards removed
- spinner with two sections labeled: smallest number and greatest number (An easy way to make a spinner is to draw a circle on a piece of paper, use a paper clip as the "arrow," and use a sharpened pencil point to hold the paper clip in place.)

Object of the Game

- to end up with all of the playing cards

Directions

- Divide the playing cards evenly among all of the players.
- At the magic word ("flip"), all players turn over their top cards. One player spins the spinner. The player with the card that matches the spinner wins the round.
- If two or more players have cards that match the spinner, those players would then turn over the next top card. Whoever of those players has the card that matches the spinner wins the round.

Variations

- Change the categories on the spinner.
- Instead of turning over one card, have the players turn over two cards to make "tens" and "ones." The first card turned over will be the "tens." The second card will be the "ones." Suggested categories: odd/even number in the ones place, odd/even number in the tens place.

Games 21 and 22

Shapes Rule!

Number of Players: 2 or more

Skills

- identifying shapes
- reading shape words

Materials

- playing board (page 27)
- marker for each player
- 20 index cards (5 for each shape) labeled with the following shape words: circle, heart, star, or arrow
- 20 index cards (5 for each shape) with pictures of circles, hearts, stars, or arrows (Magazine pictures, stamps, or stickers can also be used.)

Object of the Game

- to be crowned the Ruler of Shapes! (To win, the player must land on the arrow directly next to the crown.)

Directions

- Each player places his or her marker in the start box. Taking turns, each player turns over a card and moves his or her marker to the closest matching shape.

Don't Be Late!

Number of Players: 2 or more

Skills: reading time to the hour and to the half hour

Materials

- playing board (page 28)
- marker for each player
- 22 index cards labeled with the following times using words ("one o'clock") or numbers ("1:00") (Make a set of cards of the following times: 1:00, 1:30, 2:00, 2:30, 3:00, 3:30, 4:00, 4:30, 5:00, 5:30, 6:00, 6:30, 7:00, 7:30, 8:00, 8:30, 9:00, 9:30, 10:00, 10:30, 11:00, 11:30.)

Object of the Game

- to be the first one to catch "Tim the Timer"

Directions

- Each player places his or her marker in the start box. Taking turns, each player turns over a card and moves his or her marker to the closest matching time.

Game 21 *(cont.)*

Start →

Shapes Rule!

Be the first to be crowned the Ruler of Shapes. Place your marker at Start and spin the spinner (or pick a shapes card).

Move to the nearest matching shape. If someone else lands in your spot, you have to go back to Start. If you land in the box above the ladder, slide down —it's a shortcut!

Game 22 *(cont.)*

Place your counters at Start. Turn over a time card and move to the nearest matching clock. The first one to catch Tim the Timer wins the game. The grandfather clock is a shortcut. If you land In the box below the grandfather clock, climb up the grandfather clock to the clock above it. If another player lands in your space, you need to go back to Start!

Don't Be Late!

Start

Game 23 ✪ ꙮ ✪ ꙮ ✪ ꙮ ꙮ ✪ ꙮ ✪

Penny Toss

Number of Players: 1 or more

Skills: adding or subtracting to a given number

Materials

0	4	2	3	1
1	3	0	2	5
2	1	4	5	3
3	2	5	1	4
4	0	1	3	2

- large playing board similar to the one shown on this page (Ideas for making the playing board: use a large piece of poster board; tape together 25 sheets of blank paper; cut open a paper grocery bag and lay it flat on the ground.)
- small game markers that can be safely tossed, such as beans, paper clips, clothes pins, etc.
- scratch paper
- pencils
- *optional:* number line

Object of the Game

- to be the first player to reach a given number

Directions

- Taking turns, each player throws a marker onto the playing board. The player records the number on a piece of paper. On his or her next turn, the player throws a marker and adds the number it lands on to the number already recorded. (Each player will be keeping a running score.)

Variations

- Use different numbers to make the game easier or harder.
- Have each player take 10 turns. The player with the most points wins the game.
- A more challenging version of the game is to have each player alternate between adding and subtracting the numbers. Example: Melinda's marker lands on the following numbers: 3, 2, 5, 1, 4. She writes $3 + 2 - 5 + 1 - 4 = -3$ (in the hole). Patrick's marker lands on 5, 1, 0, 3, 3. He writes $5 + 1 - 0 + 3 - 3 = 6$. He wins the game.
- Have each player start off with the same number, such as 20. Use small numbers, such as 0–5, on the playing board. On each throw, the player subtracts the number the marker landed on from 20. The first player to reach 0 wins the game.

Game 24

Rolling Numbers

Number of Players: 1 or more

Skills
- identifying odd and even numbers
- recognizing numbers

Materials
- one playing board for each player (See the sample below.)
- three dice for each group of players

Object of the Game
- to fill one column with numbers

Directions
- Taking turns, each player rolls the dice and records the numbers in one of the following columns: Singles (three separate numbers), Doubles (two dice with the same number), Triples (all three dice with the same number), In a Row (three numbers in sequence), All Odd Numbers, All Even Numbers, Exactly 10 (All three numbers add up to ten.)

Variations
- To make the game easier, play with only a few of the categories such as: All Odd Numbers, All Even Numbers, Singles, or use two dice and eliminate the triples category.
- Have the players take 10 turns and compare the results.

2 + 5 + 6 = 13						
1 + 2 + 5 = 8	2 + 2 + 5 = 9					
2 + 3 + 7 = 12	1 + 1 + 4 = 6		2 + 3 + 4 = 9	1 + 3 + 3 = 7		
1 + 3 + 4 = 8	5 + 5 + 2 = 12	3 + 3 + 3 = 9	4 + 5 + 6 = 15	1 + 1 + 3 = 5	2 + 2 + 4 = 8	2 + 2 + 6 = 10
Singles	**Doubles**	**Triples**	**In a Row**	**All Odd Numbers**	**All Even Numbers**	**Exactly 10**

Games 25 and 26

Hundreds of Riddles

Number of Players: 1 or more

Skills
- place values (tens and ones)
- identifying even and odd numbers

Materials
- crayons
- hundreds board for each playerr

Object of the Game
- to identify the mystery number

Directions
- Have each player read the clues (page 33) or read the clues to the player. Have the player color the numbers that fit (or do not fit) the clues.

Variation
- Create original riddles using smaller sets of numbers. For example: 1–20, 50–75, 30–80, etc.

Graph Art

Number of Players: 1 or more

Skill: identifying coordinate points

Materials
- graph art pages
- crayons

Object of the Game
- to discover the mystery picture

Directions
- Have the player read each coordinate point and color the matching square the appropriate color.

Variation
- Create original Graph Art using 1" graph paper.

Game 25 *(cont.)*

Hundreds Chart

- Read the clues (page 33) to solve each hundreds riddles.
- Use beans or pennies to cover the numbers that do not fit each clue.
- Make up your own hundreds riddles to share with your family or friends.

1	2	3	4	5	6	7	8	9	10
11	12	13	14	15	16	17	18	19	20
21	22	23	24	25	26	27	28	29	30
31	32	33	34	35	36	37	38	39	40
41	42	43	44	45	46	47	48	49	50
51	52	53	54	55	56	57	58	59	60
61	62	63	64	65	66	67	68	69	70
71	72	73	74	75	76	77	78	79	80
81	82	83	84	85	86	87	88	89	90
91	92	93	94	95	96	97	98	99	100

Game 25 *(cont.)*

Hundreds of Riddles Games

Read each clue. Color the numbers that fit (or do not fit) the clue.

Riddle #1

- The mystery number has a one as one of its digits.
- It is a two-digit number.
- It has two odd numbers.
- When the two numbers are added together, the sum is 4.
- When the smaller number is subtracted from the larger number, the difference is 2.

★ **What is the mystery number?**

Riddle #2

- The mystery number is a two-digit number.
- It has two even numbers.
- When the two numbers are added together, the sum is 10.
- The number in the ones place is smaller than the number in the tens place.
- When the smaller number is subtracted from the larger number, the difference is 6.

★ **What is the mystery number?**

Riddle #3

- The mystery number is greater than 50 and less than 100.
- The mystery number has two odd numbers.
- The mystery number has two different numbers.
- When the two numbers are added together, the sum is greater than 10 and less than 16.
- The number in the ones place is larger than the number in the tens place.
- The difference between the larger number and the smaller number is 4.

★ **What is the mystery number?**

Game 26 *(cont.)*

Graph Art #1

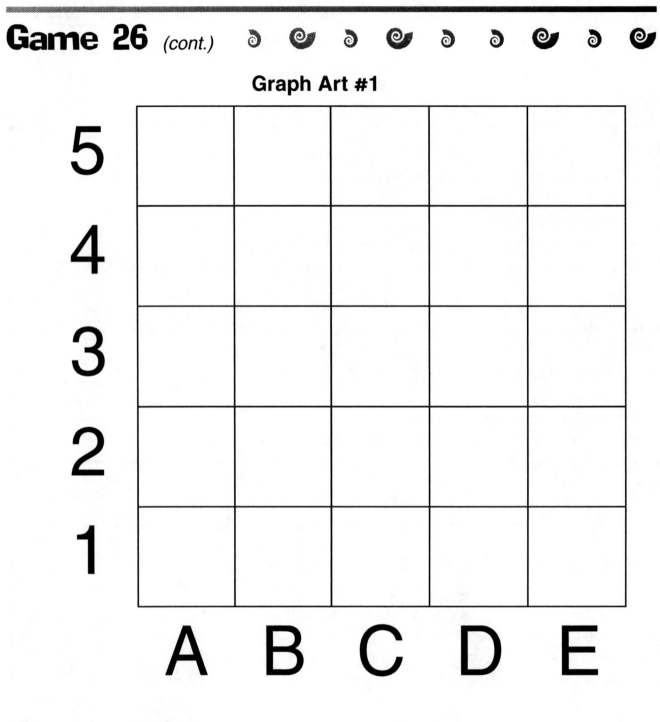

Color each part of the graph.

Yellow		
B4	B1	D4
A2	D1	C1
E2		

Orange					
E1	A4	A3	D5	C3	C2
A1	C4	E5	C5	A5	B2
D2	B5	D3	B3	E4	E3

What is the mystery picture? _____

Game 26 *(cont.)*

Graph Art #2

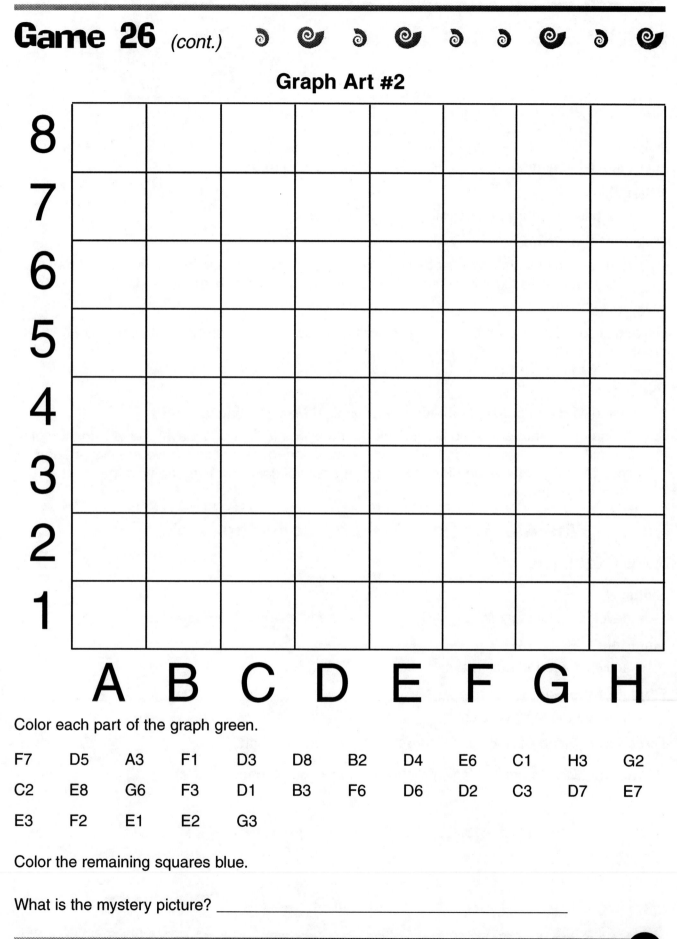

Color each part of the graph green.

F7	D5	A3	F1	D3	D8	B2	D4	E6	C1	H3	G2
C2	E8	G6	F3	D1	B3	F6	D6	D2	C3	D7	E7
E3	F2	E1	E2	G3						

Color the remaining squares blue.

What is the mystery picture? _____

Games 27 and 28

Math Art

Number of Players: 1 or more

Skills
- identifying numbers
- counting to 9

Materials
- one playing board for each player
- crayons

Object of the Game
- to use as many squares as possible in making the specific numbers (Each combination of squares used to make a number must be touching on at least one side.)

Directions

Using the specified crayon colors, the player finds and colors different combinations of numbers to reach 4, 5, 6, 7, 8, or 9.

Variations
- Using 1" graph paper, create your own original Math Art pages.
- Using one board and six different colors of crayons (3 for each player), take turns to color the different combinations of numbers. After coloring the spaces, have the player keep "score" of the total value of numbers he or she has colored. The one with the most points wins the game.

Who Ate Our Porridge! and Collectors' Collections

Number of Players: 1

Skills
- developing logical thinking skills
- reading clues for information

Materials
- activity page for each player

Object of the Game
- to solve the logic problem

Directions: Read each clue. Record the answer on the chart.

Variations: Create original logic problems using 1" graph paper.

Game 27 *(cont.)*

Math Art #1

Color two, three, or four numbers with a sum equal to 4, 5, or 6.

| 4 = red | 5 = orange | 6 = yellow |

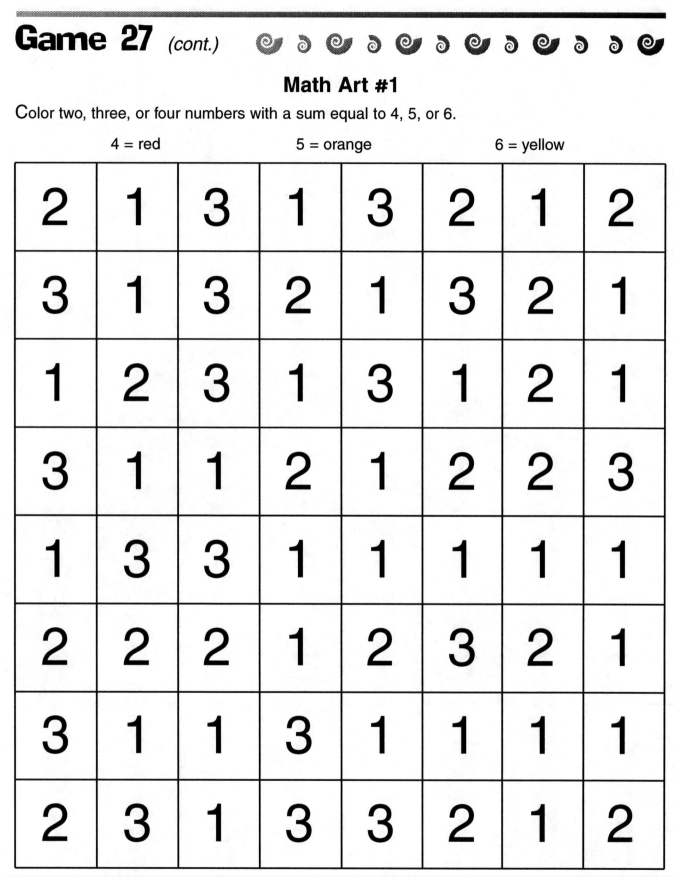

2	1	3	1	3	2	1	2
3	1	3	2	1	3	2	1
1	2	3	1	3	1	2	1
3	1	1	2	1	2	2	3
1	3	3	1	1	1	1	1
2	2	2	1	2	3	2	1
3	1	1	3	1	1	1	1
2	3	1	3	3	2	1	2

Game 27 *(cont.)*

Math Art #2

Color two, three, or four numbers with a sum equal to 7, 8, or 9.

7 = green   8 = blue   9 = purple

3	2	4	3	2	3	4	3
4	2	3	2	4	2	2	2
3	3	2	2	2	3	4	4
2	2	4	2	3	3	3	3
2	3	4	3	4	4	2	3
4	2	3	2	4	2	2	2
3	4	4	3	4	3	2	4
2	4	3	2	4	3	2	2

Game 28 *(cont.)*

Who Ate Our Porridge?

Read the clues to find out who ate the three bears' porridge.

- If the answer is "no", make an "X" in the box.
- If the answer is "yes", make an "O" in the box.

	Little Red	Goldilocks	Wolf
Baby Bear			
Mama Bear			
Papa Bear			

☆ Baby Bear's porridge was eaten in one gulp by the Big Bad Wolf.

☆ Goldilocks did not eat the Papa Bear's porridge.

Draw lines matching each person to the bear's porridge he or she ate.

| Baby Bear | Mama Bear | Papa Bear |

| Goldilocks | Little Red | Wolf |

Game 28 *(cont.)*

Collectors' Collections

Read the clues to find out what each person collects.

☆ If the answer is "no", make an "X" in the box.

☆ If the answer is "yes", make an "O" in the box.

☆ Forest collects pennies from around the world.

☆ Tracie saves the stamps from postcards and letters from around the world.

☆ Gabby does not collect teddy bears.

Draw lines matching each person to the item he or she collects.

Games 29 and 30

Shape Patterns and Finish the Patterns

Number of Players: 1

Skills

- identifying patterns
- extending a pattern

Materials

- activity pages

Object of the Activity

- to identify and extend a pattern

Directions: Have the player identify and extend a pattern.

Variations

- Create new patterns using colors, shapes, numbers, letters, stamps, and/or stickers.
- Create difficult patterns by using three or more characteristics, such as big red hearts, small red hearts, green squares, and yellow squares.

Can You Find the Mistake?

Number of Players: 1

Skills

- identifying patterns
- finding the mistakes

Materials:

- activity pages

Object of the Activity

- to find the mistake within a given pattern

Directions: Have the player identify the pattern and find the mistake within the pattern.

Variations

- Have the player rewrite the pattern correctly.
- Have the player create a pattern with one mistake. See if someone else can identify the mistake. Complete each pattern.

Game 29 *(cont.)*

Finish the Patterns

Complete each pattern.

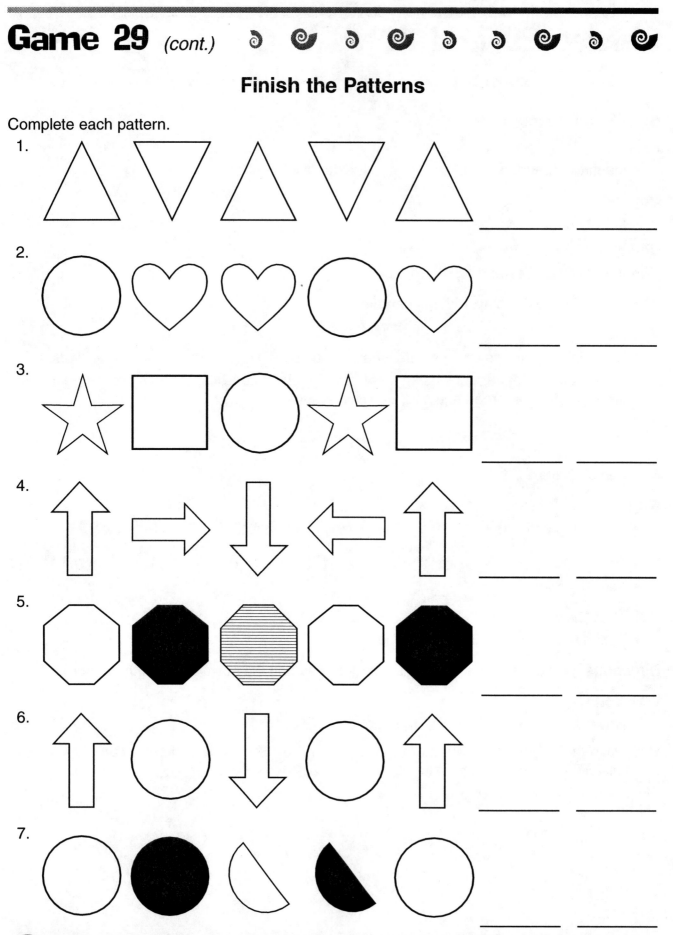

1.

2.

3.

4.

5.

6.

7.

Game 29 *(cont.)*

Finish the Patterns

Write the missing number or numbers to complete each pattern.

1.

1	2	3
	5	4

2.

7	8	9	10
	13		11

3.

1	2	3		5
3	4		6	

4.

1	2	1	3		4	1		1

5.

10	11	13	14		17	19		22

6.

1	2		4		6	7	
2		6		10			16

Patterns

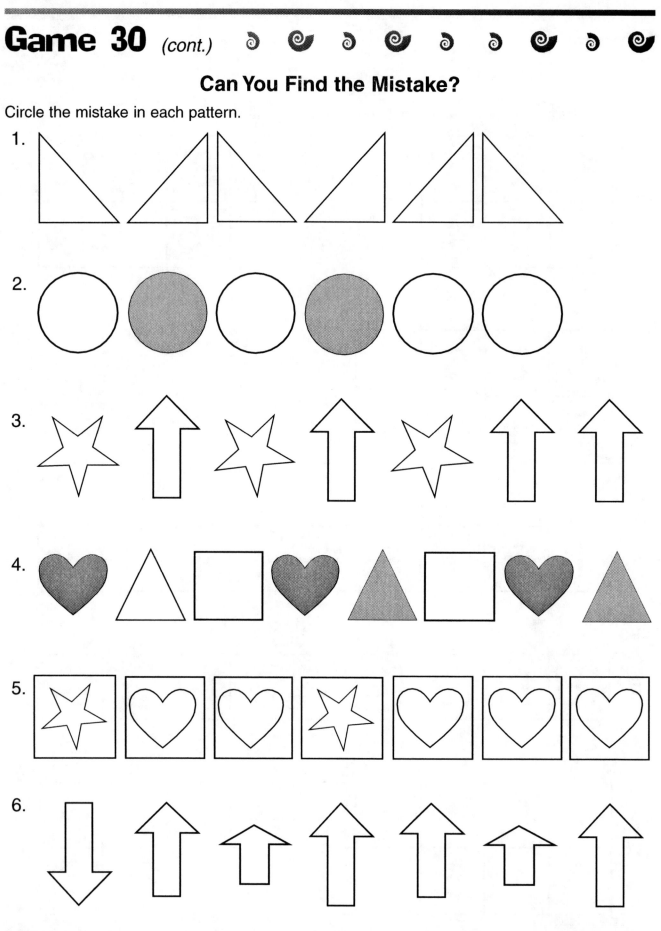

Game 30 (cont.)

Can You Find the Mistake?

Circle the mistake in each pattern.

1.

2.

3.

4.

5.

6.

© Teacher Created Resources, Inc.

Game 31

Shhh! Say It In Code #1

Number of Players: 1 or more

Skill: using letters and numbers to create a coded message

Materials
- activity pages

Object of the Game
- to solve the problem and to decode a message

Directions
- Have each player solve each math problem and then decode the message.

Variations
- Have each player develop his own code using numbers, pictures, letters, shapes, etc. Then Have the other player decode the message.

To decode the message, write the letter that goes with each shape on the line.

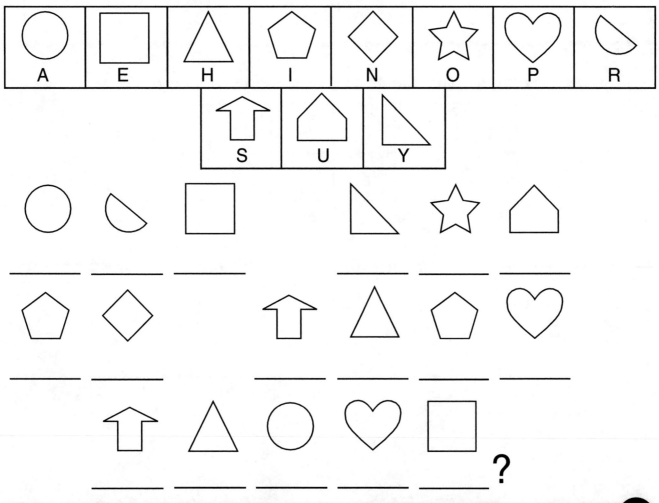

Game 31 *(cont.)*

Shhh! Say It in Code #2

Solve each math problem. Write the letter that goes with each answer in the box. Use the code to discover the answer.

What did the camera say to the mouse?

A	C	E	H	S	Y
3	1	5	2	0	4

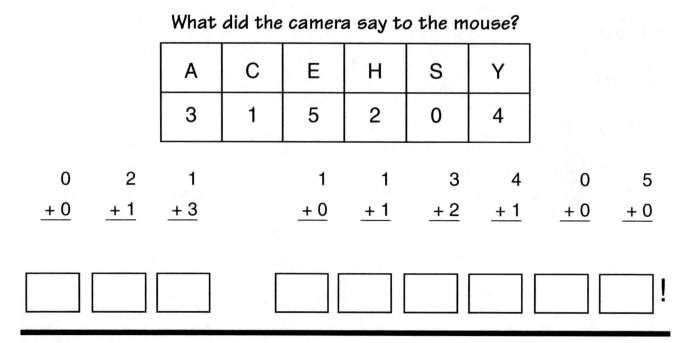

```
  0      2      1            1      1      3      4      0      5
+ 0    + 1    + 3          + 0    + 1    + 2    + 1    + 0    + 0
```

☐ ☐ ☐   ☐ ☐ ☐ ☐ ☐ ☐ !

What did the pebble say to the say to the rock?

E	L	O	R	S	T
1	4	3	0	5	2

```
  6      2      5      5            4      6      5      4
- 2    - 1    - 3    - 0          - 4    - 3    - 1    - 0
```

☐ ☐ ☐ ' ☐   ☐ ☐ ☐ ☐ !

Game 32

Build a House

Number of Players: 1 or more players

Skills

- counting money
- making change

Materials

- price list
- scratch paper
- one six-sided die pattern

Object of the Game

- to build a house within a certain price range

Directions

- Enlarge the die pattern on the right. Fold the sides to form a cube. Glue or tape the sides.
- Each player rolls the die to find out how much money can be spent to build a house.

	10¢	
30¢	40¢	20¢
	50¢	
	60¢	

House Components: Build-It-Yourself Price List

Answer Key ꩜ ꩜ ꩜ ꩜ ꩜ ꩜ ꩜ ꩜ ꩜

Page 33

Hundreds Riddle #1: 13; Hundreds Riddle #2: 82; Hundreds Riddle #3: 59

Page 34

The mystery picture is a happy face.

Page 35

The mystery picture is a sailboat.

Page 39

The Wolf ate Baby Bear's porridge. Goldilocks ate Mama Bear's porridge. Little Red Riding Hood ate Papa Bear's porridge.

Page 40

Cody collects bears. Forest collects coins. Gabby collects bugs. Tracie collects stamps.

Page 42

1. upside-down triangle, right-side up triangle
2. heart, circle
3. circle, star
4. right arrow, down arrow
5. striped octagon, white octagon
6. circle, down arrow
7. full black circle, 1/2 white circle

Page 43 (All answers read from left to right and top to bottom)

1. 6
2. 14, 12
3. 4, 5, 7
4. 1, 5
5. 16, 20
6. 3, 5, 8, 9

Page 44

1. 5th triangle and 6th triangle
2. last circle
3. last arrow
4. 1st triangle
5. last square
6. 1st arrow

Page 45

Are you in ship shape?

Page 46

1 SAY CHEESE!
2 LET'S ROLL!